Chip Carving

Design & Pattern Sourcebook

Wayne Barton

STERLING PUBLISHING CO., INC.
New York

With love and gratitude to my wife, Marlies, and to my children, Blaise, Teak, Cleve, and Heidi, trusting they will be ever mindful that all their hopes, wishes, and dreams are possible.

Library of Congress Cataloging-in-Publication Data

Barton, Wayne.
    Chip carving : design & pattern sourcebook / Wayne Barton.
      p. cm.
    Includes index.
    ISBN 0-8069-4403-X
    1. Wood-carving. 2. Wood-carving--Patterns. I. Title.

TT199.7 .B363 2002
736'.4--dc21   2001044677

Book design: Judy Morgan
Editor: Rodman Pilgrim Neumann

10 9 8 7 6 5 4 3

Published by Sterling Publishing Company, Inc.
387 Park Avenue South, New York, N.Y. 10016
© 2002 by Wayne Barton
Distributed in Canada by Sterling Publishing
^c/o Canadian Manda Group, One Atlantic Avenue, Suite 105
Toronto, Ontario, Canada M6K 3E7
Distributed in Great Britain by Chrysalis Books
64 Brewery Road, London N7 9NT, England
Distributed in Australia by Capricorn Link (Australia) Pty. Ltd.
P.O. Box 704, Windsor, NSW 2756 Australia
Printed in China
All rights reserved

Sterling ISBN 0-8069-4403-X

Contents

Acknowledgments

This book was inspired by the encouragement and suggestion of many of my carving friends and students. I am grateful to all who expressed a desire to see more of my patterns published. Among them I would like to mention Bruce Nicholas, Scott Phillips, David Cruthers, Don Peters, Claude Michaelson, and Dr. Harvey Morgan. I would like to give special mention to Robert A. Ostmann for many hours sharing and discussing his insights, which are clear, precise, and noteworthy. Time spent with Bob and his wife Jean is always too short.

Any acknowledgment would be incomplete without mentioning my many years of invaluable collaboration and friendship with Gottlieb Brandli, the finest of cabinetmakers and dearest of friends. He has freely shared his time and extraordinary knowledge of wood, craftsmanship, and design, always with a good sense of humor. His friendship is truly a treasure.

In terms of production, I'd like to thank my dear friend and secretary, Joanne Inda, who corrects more than my spelling. She has kindly given much extra time to see this project through. Acknowledgment must be given to my editor, Rodman Pilgrim Neumann, for his superb effort and accomplishment in arranging the material submitted to him for this book. His suggestions and editorial skills have rendered this work more easily understood. Also, a special thanks to my son, Cleve, for his invaluable expertise and assistance photographing and producing the pictures of this book. It was a father's joy having the opportunity to observe his extraordinary talents performed so professionally and pleasantly.

Most of all, I'd like to express love and gratitude to my wife, Marlies, whose patience, encouragement, and sacrifices have played an enormous role in the creation of this book. She is my best critic. Her vision is sharp when mine is not. So often her steadfast and cheerful moral support has been just what was needed for me to push forward. Thanks, again, Marlies, as always.

Introduction

The essence of chip carving is simplicity and versatility. It is a decorative style of carving quickly and is easily learned. Simple in tool use and execution; versatile in design possibilities, application, and beauty; its name is derived from the carving process rather than the end product as in character carving (shaving with hand tools) or bird carving (grinding wood away with power tools). In chip carving, precise cuts are incised into the wood forming chips of various geometric shape, size, and proportion. Design aside, good chip carving is distinguished by single-angle smooth facets, clean grooves, and sharp ridges.

Nearly every country or region has an indigenous style of chip carving, both in tools used and design, including some islands of the South Pacific. Chip carving in hard woods traditionally is done with chisels and mallet. Softer woods can be carved with knives alone. The woods employed for the carvings herein are primarily basswood (genus *Tilia*) and butternut (*Juglans cinera*); not so much for their softness alone, but for their straight, tight grain.

The carvings were done with only two knives designed specifically for chip carving, making the process efficient and pleasant. They are available from most carving tool suppliers and are highly recommended. If you experience difficulty locating them, contact the author (see the end of "Tools & Materials").

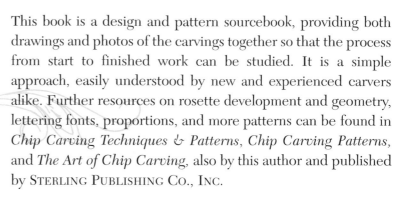

This book is a design and pattern sourcebook, providing both drawings and photos of the carvings together so that the process from start to finished work can be studied. It is a simple approach, easily understood by new and experienced carvers alike. Further resources on rosette development and geometry, lettering fonts, proportions, and more patterns can be found in *Chip Carving Techniques & Patterns*, *Chip Carving Patterns*, and *The Art of Chip Carving*, also by this author and published by STERLING PUBLISHING CO., INC.

Individual elements of design such as geometric forms, free-form motifs, and lettering are readily recognized and easily set into categories. But the lines of demarcation rapidly begin to blur when these components are combined. This is particularly true when geometric and natural or organic forms are used together in the style known as positive image. Here, rather than incising the design into the wood, the background is removed—much as it is in relief carving—but the removal of the ground is executed using the precise techniques of chip carving.

The positive-image approach vastly extends the parameters of chip carving to dimensions that are evolutionary, expansive, and exciting. It also makes ascribing carving designs to a single style category a bit difficult. Because this is so, some carvings that are shown in one category may have elements of design that could easily have placed the work in another category. They have been placed at the author's discretion and specific elements of a larger piece may appear in different categories of style.

The mechanical skills of chip carving are easily learned just by carving. The visual skills needed to create designs are acquired through observation and application. Studying and carving the designs in this sourcebook will raise your ability and awareness on both levels. Most of all, it will provide you with many pleasant hours of carving enjoyment and personal satisfaction in creating your own treasured carvings. I wish everyone using this resource great success and joy.

Notes on Design

The ability to understand and create design is within all of us. Writing is an example of how design is understood and copied. Our interpretation of letters is the creative aspect of the process.

What exactly is design? In the consideration of chip carving (as well as many other disciplines), design may be described as resolving or defining space by arranging geometric shapes, patterns, and motifs usually in a pleasing manner based on certain principles and concepts. As music has auditory rhythm, there is a visual rhythm and flow to good design. This is accomplished by line alone. A dash and a dot are recognized as segments of a line. The elements of composition, which incorporate basic geometric shapes, such as triangles, circles, and squares, also include the concepts of contrast, balance, proportion, focal point, and movement.

Because we recognize objects by their "outline," the quality (length, direction) and quantity (number) of all lines is significant. A single dot will alter the impact of design. The analysis of lines that define or represent objects usually takes place at the subconscious level. Without knowing why, we will determine whether we like or dislike a design based upon memorized feelings and experiences. To understand how and why lines affect our preferences and interpretations, we need to bring the elements of design composition to the conscious level.

When considering design for our purpose, a line may be described as having four attitudes: horizontal, vertical, diagonal, and curved. Each conveys a particular expression to which we respond because of our interpretation of past experiences or learned symbols. Combined, they form the geometric shapes and suggestions that are the foundation of decorative design.

- **Horizontal lines** represent rest and tranquility, a strong base, stability, and steadiness. **Vertical lines** also represent stability. They are the opposite of and complement the horizontal line perfectly by forming with it squares and rectangles, the two basic geometric shapes of nearly all architectural structure. Vertical lines additionally represent awareness and alertness and have an uplifting quality as observed in Gothic architecture.

- **Diagonal lines** are in transitional movement between vertical and horizontal stability, thereby expressing the exertion of energy, a force of life. The visual energy and movement expressed by a diagonal line may be subtle or severe depending on its angle.

- **Curved lines** represent constant movement of various degrees determined by the radius, expressed perfectly by a circle.

Elements of Composition

Contrast, balance, proportion, focal point, and movement assist in arranging lines and shapes so that they are visually pleasing. Knowing and recognizing these elements is essential to creating good design.

- **Contrast**—Things are often defined by what they are not, i.e., their opposites. The uncarved area of a chip carved piece defines that which is carved. This is contrast. At times it is appropriate to have all lines or chips the same in a motif to produce a particular effect or feeling as found in many borders. But if this is contrasted within the overall design—large and small, straight and curved, square and round, etc.—the composition is extended to another level. Contrast within a composition will cause a carving to be more compelling.

- **Balance** is counterpoise, an equilibrium, an arrangement wherein opposing forces neutralize each other. Visual balance can, but need not, be symmetrical. A seven-point rosette is considered asymmetrical but is easily placed in a balanced position. Baroque architecture exemplifies the complete rejection of symmetry but is in perfect visual balance. No matter what other elements are brought into a design, visual balance will create steadiness.

- **Proportion** is related to balance through equipoise, a visual weighting in size, number, and distance of the various parts of a design. When symmetrical, proportion demands that the parts be equal in all ways. When asymmetrical, the parts need be of a proportion to each other to maintain visual balance.

- **Focal point** refers to that place or area to where the eye is first drawn naturally and continues to return as it takes in the entire design. Nearly always this will be the center of a piece. It may be a dot, a letter or letters, a circle, or a complete rosette. It dominates the composition simply or elaborately and all else complements and supports it.

- **Movement,** created by diagonal and curved lines, adds excitement and energy to a composition. Diagonal lines may form triangles or diamonds while curves may form circles and ovals.

Design Suggestions

Being consciously aware of the elements of design, their effect and interpretation, will greatly assist in their incorporation. Awareness is the key.

- Create chips that are carvable. Don't make them too large for the thickness of the wood to be carved.

- Leave visual breathing space. Usually it is not a good idea to carve every millimeter of wood in a design. Sometimes simplicity is best.

- Placing a border too close to the edge of a piece often will cause the carving to appear cramped and ill-conceived.

- Create chips that relate to, and complement, each other. They should not appear as though they are floating aimlessly.

- To achieve a visual third dimension effect, avoid assigning the same value to all the lines (chips) to be carved. Vary the width of your lines.

- A design is best when not "read" in a moment's glance. Employing the various elements and concepts of design will create interest. The visual communication between the artist and audience is, and should be, a joyful, enduring encounter.

Tools & Materials

One of the unexpected pleasures of chip carving is the discovery of the limited number of tools and materials needed to do truly fine carving. And, unlike some other forms of carving, acquiring additional tools will not increase your skill or produce a better finished product.

CARVING TOOLS

Ever since man has taken up woodcarving, the type of tools used has been dictated by the finished work desired and the type of wood to be carved. This holds true for all styles and methods including chip carving.

In the Middles Ages (as in some parts of the world today), chip carving was and is executed in both hard and soft woods. When hard woods are used (meaning woods that are physically hard), skews, chisels, and mallet serve best. Skews and chisels may also be used on soft wood with hand pressure alone. It is interesting to note that the softer the wood is, the sharper the tool must be. Dull tools will crush rather than cut soft wood fibers, while at the same time they will "bite" into harder wood.

Today, most chip carving is done in woods that can be cut fairly easily by knives. This makes the process faster, easier, and more available to those who desire to carve because of its simplicity, both in tools used and style employed. Knives, however, vary in quality and configuration.

The only carving tools required are a knife for cutting chips and a stab knife for making an impression as desired in the work.

Premier Chip-Carving Knives

The carvings in this book were executed with only two knives. They are the WB Premier chip-carving No. 1 cutting knife and the WB Premier No. 2 stab knife. Their design is the result of many years of carving and teaching. These tools offer improvements over those most used for years and others available today for several reasons.

Chip-carving knives designed by Wayne Barton: (Bottom) WB Premier No. 1 cutting knife; (Top) WB Premier No. 2 stab knife.

One is that the blades are made of high-carbon true tool steel, not stainless. Another is the greater downward angle of the No. 1 cutting knife. The tip of this blade is more sharply pointed, allowing the carver to make curved cuts more easily as well as execute tighter corners and niches. The No. 2 stab knife has a longer blade edge, allowing longer "stabs" to be made, increasing the design possibilities.

Another significant advantage of these knives is their ergonomically designed handles. The handles have been shaped from domestic wood, allowing for a good grip and hours of comfortable, easy, nonfatiguing carving. A more satisfying handle will be hard to find. When only two knives are used, give yourself every advantage. Cheap inadequate tools produce only disappointing results, and often are a waste of time and money.

The WB Premier No. 1 cutting knife is used to remove all wood chips. The WB Premier No. 2 stab knife is used to decorate and complement the work done by the cutting knife. The stab knife removes no wood at all; instead it cuts and spreads the wood, making permanent indented impressions of any variety of lengths, combinations, and designs. Although most work is done with the cutting knife, it is a mistake to disregard the capabilities of the stab knife. Students who neglect the stab knife deny themselves the full possibilities of chip carving.

Tools needed for chip carving: pencil, eraser, T-square ruler, draftsman's compass, cutting and stab chip carving knives, and ceramic sharpening and polishing stones.

Other Tools for Chip Carving

The remainder of the tools needed for chip carving are a pencil (a mechanical one with a 0.05 lead size works well), eraser, T-square ruler, drafting- or bow-type compass, and ceramic sharpening and polishing stones. Use a grade "B" lead for both the compass and pencil. This softer-grade lead makes legible lines without impressing the wood, and it is easier to clean off than the harder grades of lead. When it is time to clean all of the excess pencil marks off your carving, you'll find that an ink eraser does it quickly and neatly.

Safety

With quality tools and their proper use, chip carving is a safe and satisfying carving experience. Use common sense and develop good habits when carving.

Although you may have a table or workbench upon which to set your tools or your work, chip carving is best done with the maximum amount of control and leverage, which means doing all of your work in your lap. With your elbows close to your body, you will have added leverage and strength from your shoulders. Unless the workpiece is too large to hold, sitting at a table or workbench forfeits your leverage and strength.

Overhead fluorescent lights are generally poor for carving, because they diffuse the light making it "shadowless." When not using natural light, use a shaded single 100-watt bulb below eye level to cut glare. It will give you hard, sharp shadows that are easily seen for better carving.

Working with Chip-Carving Knives

Keep your tools sharp, as described below under "Sharpening." Keep your work clean and crisp. Don't leave little bits of wood in the bottom of your cuts.

Holding your knives properly may seem awkward at first but, with practice, they will become quite familiar to you. The stab knife is held with one or two hands perpendicular to the work. It is thrust downward to make an impression of the desired depth and length.

The cutting knife is used in two positions. The first position is used for all line cuts, straight and curved, as well as for the first and third cuts of small, regular triangular chips. The second position is used only for the second cut of the triangular chips. Some part of your hand is always touching the work as a guide, at all times, when using the cutting knife.

For the first position, hold the cutting knife in your right hand (left-handed carvers like the author, simply reverse the process). Place the joint of your thumb (curved outward) at the end of the handle by the blade on the lower inside of the handle. The thumb and knuckles should rest on the work. The po-

sition is similar to holding a knife to peel potatoes, except that the thumb should never leave the handle.

For the second position, the thumb is moved directly on top of the outside spine of the handle, with the first knuckle of the thumb still next to the blade, not on it. The two positions give the same (proper) angle for carving in opposing directions.

Make all cuts only as deep as is necessary to remove a chip, avoiding excessive undercutting. Ideally, you only make a cut once. In the case of larger chips, it may be advantageous to first remove the top half of the chip, and then go back to get the rest. A too-deep cut may split your workpiece, if the pressure is not relieved in this way. Remember to keep part of your hand or finger touching the work as a guide when using the cutting knife—or you will have no control.

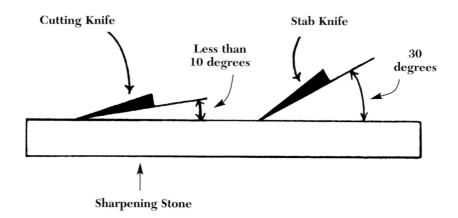

Angles for sharpening cutting and stab knives.

Sharpening Chip Carving Knives

The lack of a sharp edge to your tools can deprive you of the joy of carving. There are three criteria to the process of sharpening: sharpening at the correct angle, producing a sharp cutting edge, and producing a blade that is polished.

Chip carving, unlike all other forms of carving, which are executed by shaving wood, calls for the carver to insert the blade into the wood to remove specific shapes, pieces or chips. The angle at which the blade is sharpened is critical but not impossible to achieve.

Flat ceramic sharpening stones (not rods) are best. They are so hard that even with extended use they remain flat. Unlike natural stones, the high quality of the ceramic stone is uniform and constant. Further, the ceramic stone requires no oil or water as lubricant in the sharpening process.

You need both a medium-grade and an ultra-fine stone. The angle of the properly sharpened edge is approximately 10 degrees or less. You can gauge the maximum angle by raising the knife off the stone just until a dime (U.S. 10-cent coin) can be slipped under the back edge of the blade. In many cases you will want an angle less than this.

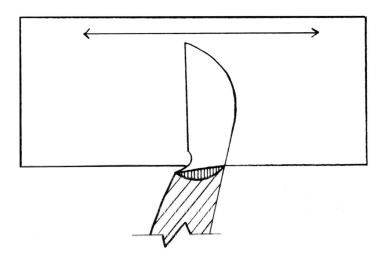

Slide the knife blade back and forth across the stone to sharpen.

Sharpen the cutting knife first on the medium-grade stone, keeping equal pressure on the heel and tip of the blade. A back-and-forth movement with pressure on one side, and then equally of the other works well. Bring the edge to a slight burr. Continue as before but with less pressure until the burr disappears. Check light reflection by holding the knife under a bright light with your finger on the tip, to cut any glare. When there is no burr and you see no light reflecting off the edge, the knife is ready for polishing.

Use the ultra-fine ceramic stone to hone each side equally so that you don't create a burr. Polishing the metal in this way will assure that the blade will glide easily through the wood rather than drag.

Check for light reflection again, and cut diagonally across the grain of a piece of scrap wood to check for drag. Your knife should flow smoothly and steadily.

The stab knife is sharpened with the same stones and procedures used for the cutting knife, with the exception of the sharpening angle. The angle for the stab knife is approximately 30 degrees. Because the stab knife is used only for impressing or indenting the wood to enhance a design, the angle of the cutting edge is more crucial than its sharpness.

The frequency of sharpening will depend on the quality of the steel in your blades, the variety of wood being used, and the type of cuts being made. Some kinds of wood can dull a blade quickly, and deep and curved cuts can wear an edge in no time.

You will develop a feel for when it is time to hone your blades on the ultra-fine stone. You will find yourself using more pressure to get the same results than you did initially. Also, you will notice that light begins to reflect from the edge as it dulls. To freshen the edges, normally using only the ultra-fine stone will suffice to sharpen the cutting edge.

SELECTION OF WOOD

Not all types of wood can be used effectively for chip carving with knives, and some are better than others. There are several criteria to consider in selecting wood for carving.

"The tighter and straighter the grain the better" is a general guide for chip carving. Open-grain woods have a tendency to split and limit the intricacy of the design. Irregularly grained woods lessen your control of the cut, making accuracy more difficult. Highly figured and exotic grained woods tend to obscure carving and are generally hard. Softer, unspectacular, straight-grained wood works best.

All of the carvings shown herein are executed in basswood, butternut, or Eastern white pine. These woods, particularly basswood (also referred to as linden or lime), are exceptionally well suited for chip carving, although they are not the only ones that carve well. Jelutong, catalpa, buckeye, tupelo, cypress, mahogany, and black willow can also be used.

Suitable Woods for Chip Carving

❧ **Basswood** is an easy and satisfying wood to carve. It is pale cream to yellowish brown with a uniform fine texture. Basswood is essentially identical to what Europeans know as linden/lime. Linden is a family of trees—*Tiliaceae*—of which the genus *Tilia* is generally termed linden, native in temperate regions. The North American linden (*Tilia americana*) is commonly referred to as "basswood" or "whitewood." This close-grained wood is most satisfying for any chip-carving project. Northern-grown basswood seems to perform better than southern.

❧ **Butternut** (*Juglans cinera*) is a hardwood sometimes also called white walnut. The heartwood is a light brown, frequently with pinkish tones or darker brown streaks. It is moderately light in weight (about the same as eastern white pine), rather coarse-textured, and moderately soft. It resembles black walnut, especially when stained. Like basswood, butternut is a joy to carve.

❧ **Eastern white pine** (*Pinus strobus*) is sometimes confused with Ponderosa pine (*Pinus ponderosa*) and western white (*Pinus monticola*), and also known in some areas as Weymouth pine as well as by other names. This is a straight-grained, even-textured softwood that is good for chip carving, although it tends to split. The heartwood is light brown, often with a reddish tinge; exposure to air darkens the wood. Eastern white pine is inexpensive yet easy to work, and takes a polish well.

Finding the Materials & Tools

The materials and tools recommended and shown in this book, including the basswood plates and boxes, are generally available from most woodcarving suppliers.

Should you have difficulty finding them, contact the author for specific suppliers.

Wayne Barton
The Alpine School of Woodcarving, Ltd.
225 Vine Avenue
Park Ridge, IL 60068
847-692-2822 or fax 847-692-6626
www.chipcarving.com

Understanding the Drawings

Because of the nature of the designs, the drawings in this book are in three formats. The styles of line drawings, line shading, and solid or dark shading are selected for their simplicity and to provide greater clarity for the reader. In some instances, more than one style is given within the same drawing.

Line drawing.

In the line drawings, the part of the original surface of the wood that is left after carving is outlined with simple lines. To understand where the cuts are made to remove chips requires study of the photograph of the finished work.

Line shading.

In the line shading drawings, the shaded areas correspond to where chips are removed. Occasionally the shaded area will have lines running through them that may indicate ridges that will be preserved when the wood is cut away to either side. By studying the companion photo of the carved design, the nuances in the transition from drawing to finished carving may be more readily understood.

Solid or dark shading.

The solid or dark shaded area corresponds to the recessed area where chips have been removed. The area left unshaded is the flat surface left from the original piece of wood.

Laying Out & Transferring Patterns

Laying out all of the basic lines of a design before carving will ensure that the finished work will be proportionally correct and visually balanced. Whether the shape of the piece to be carved is round or square, begin by quartering it. This will locate the exact center and provide the basis for all other divisions. If the design is entirely geometric, all or most of it can be easily drawn directly on the wood with the aid of a compass and ruler.

When a non-geometric design, such as foliage, is to be transferred, put it first on tracing paper. Use graphite paper when transferring the pattern onto the wood. Trace with a nonmarking stylus to maintain the integrity of the original design. The

First step — transferring the pattern to the wood.

use of carbon paper should be avoided for this step since the colored wax transmitted from this material can permanently stain the wood.

It is not recommended to glue the pattern on the wood and carve through the paper. While this may appear to be a short-cut in preparation to carve, it has serious drawbacks. It is impossible to see through the paper in the process of carving. Wood may be cut or cracked out that was not intended to be removed. Even if a transparent paper is used, the same result may occur and not be discovered until the paper is removed. Having the paper move or come loose during carving is also a concern. Removing adhesive after the paper is lifted is not only bothersome, but raises the possibility of damaging the carving.

A photocopy may be transferred by placing it face down on the wood and ironing the back side of the paper with a very hot iron. The ease of sizing the pattern to fit is a benefit, but, beware that with this technique the pattern is reversed, and the ironed-on lines may be more difficult to clean up than pencil lines or marks made left by graphite paper. The toner of a photocopier may also be released by applying a cloth dampened with lacquer thinner to the back side of the paper.

Lettering

Lettering has always been a natural part of chip carving, from individual letters on jewelry or music boxes to names and extensive quotations for commemorative items, signs, chests, and even buildings. The fastest and easiest way to carve letters is the incised method employed in chip carving.

The method used to carve letters is the same as that used in executing all other chip carving, i.e., the way the knife is held and chips are removed. Lettering is easily executed because the carving is done in a consistent manner; a single-edged knife is held in a constantly locked position and drawn forward.

Any number of lettering styles or fonts is available for carving. Some, of course, are much easier to execute and lend themselves to chip carving more than others. Attractive and easily readable, block or Roman letters, are straightforward to carve. A more fancy style of script may be suitable to become part of a flowing design.

The real criteria for selecting a font is not only how easily it may be carved, but also how well the lettering style complements the rest of the carving. Also, the letter size should be proportionate and complementary to the overall composition. The lettering shown here offers some styles and applications.

Simple letters forming a monogram within a positive-image foliage framework. Box lid, 6$^{11}/_{16}$" × 9$^{3}/_{8}$".

This study of variations of the letter B suggests that any number of lettering styles or fonts might be suitable for chip carving. Ornate letters, such as the Old English style at the middle left, work well as initials because they are strong and bold, but might be too ornate for full words.

An exaggerated
Z initial is used in
an oval, placed
within a positive-
image foliage
framework.
Basswood box lid,
9⅜" × 6¾".

*An initial S
has been
developed with
a foliated design
to complement
the positive-image
foliage framework.
Basswood box lid,
5" × 7".*

Using the positive-image foliage design as a starting point, a foliated alphabet can be created.

More examples of a foliated alphabet using a positive-image foliage design.

A positive-image foliated B is set within a geometric border framework. Butternut box lid, 5" × 5".

A foliated style of lettering is integrated within a positive image foliage design. Basswood bench brush, 12" × 1¾".

(Collection of Dr. Harvey Morgan)

Becker lettering, with upper and lower case, is complemented by a scalloped border design and a floral motif. Butternut box lid, 5" × 7".

*Ambrosia lettering with garland border. Front
panel of basswood box, 12" × 5", dated 1991.*

(Crigler collection)

*Ambrosia lettering with a positive-image foliage
border design. (See page 127 for border pattern.)
Basswood door plaque, 22" × 7".*

(Nussbaum collection)

Ambrosia lettering
set within a
positive-image
foliage framework.
Inside lid cover of
butternut box,
15" × 9",
dated 1998.

(Slickenmeyer collection)

*Altered Becker lettering. Front panel of
basswood box, 12" × 2½", dated 1996.*

(Collection of S. Pippen)

*Becker lettering with a positive-image
foliage design defining the plate border.
(See page 140 for eagle pattern.)
Basswood plate, 16", dated 1992.*

(Collection of H. Huggler-Wyss Woodcarving Shop,
Brienz, Switzerland)

Hourglass design integrates altered Becker lettering with foliated and free-form positive-image elements. Basswood plaque, 12" × 9".

Script lettering, with upper and lower case, set in a positive-image foliage framework with a button-and-dartborder design.
Inside lid cover of butternut box,8½" × 14½".

Becker lettering, with upper and lower case, expresses a phrase within a free-form floral border. Inside lid cover of basswood lap desk, 16½" × 14".

Rambling lettering forms an extended quote from "As You Like It" by William Shakespeare. Basswood plaque with bark, 32" × 14", dated 1997.

Geometric Design

The most traditional style of chip carving incorporates geometric design, often presented within or as a rosette. This is mainly for the reason that rosettes are easily drawn entirely with a compass and straightedge. Geometric designs within a circle or rosette often appear in the form of what may be called a flower for the petal-like design produced with the compass. However, they may become a bit more complicated and intricate by imposing one geometric form upon or within another. One can discover a multitude of design possibilities.

Basic geometric shapes, such as the square, diamond, rectangle, and star, can be put together with or without the circle in any number of ways. Geometric elements often form borders or are part of a design with foliated and free-form elements.

With few exceptions, most geometric designs are balanced by carved and uncarved areas. One will define the other. It is easy and sometimes tempting to carve a space just because it is there. When designing, give consideration to the overall balance and "readability" of the design. It works best when the carving is readily understood. For some of the examples of designs and patterns in this section, the geometric component of the larger work has been isolated to help clarify its design. The full context of the isolated elements can be studied in the following section, Designs for Cabinets/Furniture.

*Detail of door
panel, 5" rosette,
butternut.*

*Detail of door panel,
5" rosette, butternut.*

Detail of door panel, 5" rosette, butternut.

Detail of door panel,
5" rosette, butternut.

Detail of door panel,
5" rosette, butternut.

Detail of door panel, 5" rosette, butternut.

Detail of box lid, 5" rosette, butternut.

5" snowflake ornament, basswood.

*5" snowflake
ornament,
basswood.*

*5" snowflake
ornament,
basswood.*

*5" snowflake ornament,
basswood.*

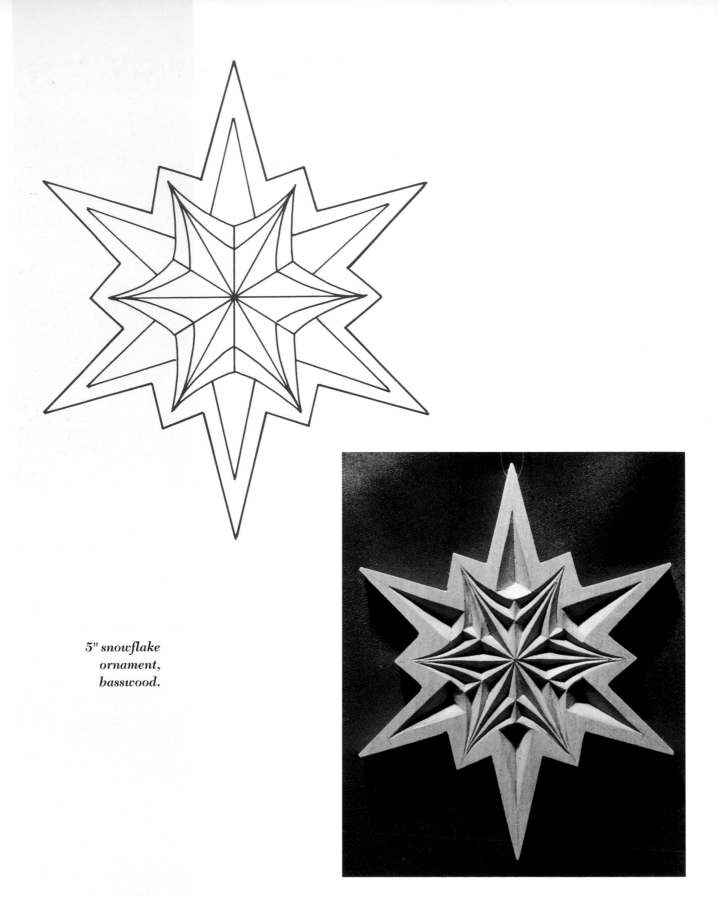

*5" snowflake
ornament,
basswood.*

*5" snowflake
ornament,
basswood.*

Geometric rosette positive-image border,
12" scalloped beaded-rim plate, basswood.

A collection of
6" scoop plates,
basswood.

*6" scoop plate,
basswood.*

10" rim plate, basswood.

*10" scalloped
rim plate,
basswood.*

16" scalloped rim plate, basswood.

Detail of rosette.

Pattern for 10" rim plate.

*10" rim plate,
basswood.*

**Geometric rosette with multiple positive-image borders,
12¾" × 8¼" box lid, basswood.**

(Crigler collection)

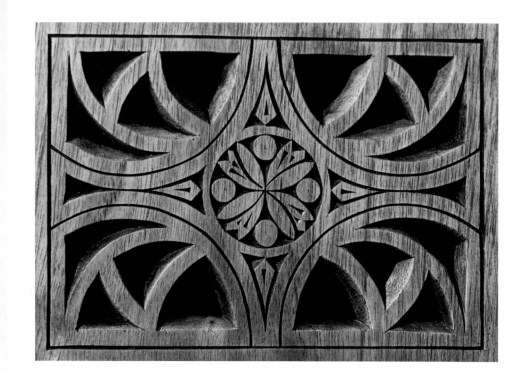

*Pierced cover
for music box,
6½" × 5",
butternut.*

*Balancing wine
bottle holder,
12" × 3½".*

Cribbage board with scalloped edges and initials HB, dated 1998, 14½" × 5", basswood.

Gothic rosette design, 3" diameter.

Octagonal lamp base,
11" × 5½".

Rosette detail of
lamp base,
1¾" diameter.

Rosette detail of lamp base, 1¾" diameter.

*Rosette detail of lamp base,
1¾" diameter.*

*Rosette detail of lamp base,
1¾" diameter.*

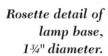

*Rosette detail of
lamp base,
1¾" diameter.*

*Box lid,
5" × 5",
basswood.*

Front panel of lap desk,
16½" × 6", basswood.

Side panel of lap desk,
14" × 6", basswood.

Side panel of lap desk,
14" × 6", basswood.

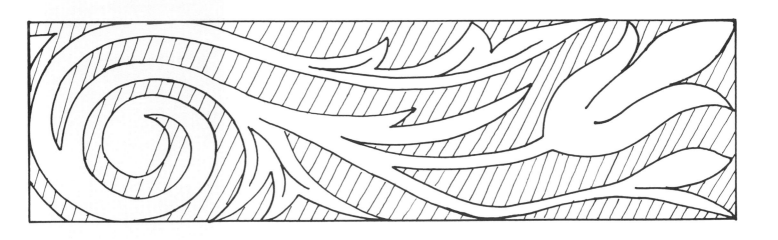

Front panel of lap desk,
16½" × 6", basswood.

*15th century
Norman Gothic
hearth stool.*

Trestle of hearth stool.

*Top of hearth stool with
geometric scallopped lace
and foliage patterns.*

*Side panel of
hearth stool,
foliage design
with geometric
rosette center.*

*Inside leg of
hearth stool.*

12" scalloped rim plate, basswood.

Designs for Cabinets/Furniture

This section shows the application of all forms and styles of chip carving including geometric, free form, and positive image applied to furniture and cabinets. This is an excellent use of chip carving, being a decorative style of carving. The objects themselves, whether they be chair backs or door panels, merely present the shape or form to be considered for design. It is important to give consideration to the entire object and where it is to be seen when selecting your pattern. If it is a single item, such as a chair, the shape of the chair and where it will be placed and among what other objects should be taken into account when selecting a pattern. If a door panel is to be carved, consideration of all other panels and the overall effect becomes important. Furthermore, distance from which the carving is generally to be viewed is also a factor.

Generally, furniture and cabinet projects are larger undertakings than most chip carving projects, offering more irregular shapes. Don't let their size and/or complexity put you off. They can prove to be some of your most rewarding pieces.

Kitchen cabinet doors, 31" × 14" each, butternut.

Door panel details.

Door panel details.

Kitchen cabinet doors, 17" × 17" each, butternut.

Kitchen cabinet door, 13" × 9", door panel detail.

*Kitchen
cabinet door
panel pattern.*

Kitchen cabinet door panel pattern.

Kitchen cabinet door, 17" × 12", door panel detail.

Kitchen cabinet doors,
18" × 13".

Door panel detail.

Kitchen cabinet drawer with door panels.

Door panel detail.

Kitchen cabinet door,
15¾" × 6¼".

Kitchen cabinet door, 31" × 7".

Kitchen cabinet panel,
17" × 14".

*"Green Man"
kitchen cabinet
panel detail.*

Swiss style kitchen chair, white pine, free-form pattern with rosette and letter B.

Chair back, front side free-form pattern with rosette and letter B.

Reverse side of chair back, white pine, dated 1999.

Positive Image Designs

Generally speaking, any chip carving that produces a recognizable form in a relieved state (not incised), such as a bird, animal, or flower, would be classified as having a positive image. In traditional chip carving, certain executions of rosettes automatically produce a positive image. This, however, is more a result of the geometric characteristics of the rosette than original intention.

Geometric shapes, such as triangles and diamonds as well as circles, act as excellent framework for designing positive images within. However, positive-image designs are not limited to the confined form of geometric shapes. They may also be drawn and executed freely on their own. When designing foliage, try to let it appear as though it is growing out of its framework, creating a feeling of energy or organic life. This appearance is accomplished by having the leaves, lobes, and stems bend and curl against the framework, forcing them back and over, filling the entire space.

The most important consideration in a positive-image carving is that the chips you design be of the size and shape that can be executed. Though some of the chips will be similar to what is usually found in traditional geometric chip carving, many will be irregular. The same chip carving techniques are used to remove both.

Lid of jewelry box, 14½" × 8½", butternut.

*"The Prince"
wall plaque,
12" × 18",
butternut.
Positive-image
foliage and frog.
Center rosette is
incised free-form.*

*Front panel of music/jewelry box,
14½" × 6", butternut.*

Music/jewelry box lid, 14½" × 8½", butternut.

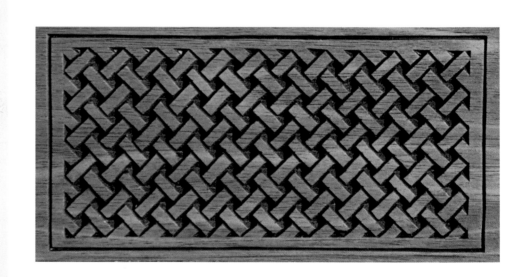

*Side panel of
music/jewelry box,
8½" × 6",
butternut.*

Lid of box with positive-image initial and center foliage design. Border includes free-form and geometric elements, 12¾" × 8½", basswood.

(S. Pippin collection)

12" scalloped-rim plate, butternut.

*Positive-image
box lid pattern,
6½" × 4½".*

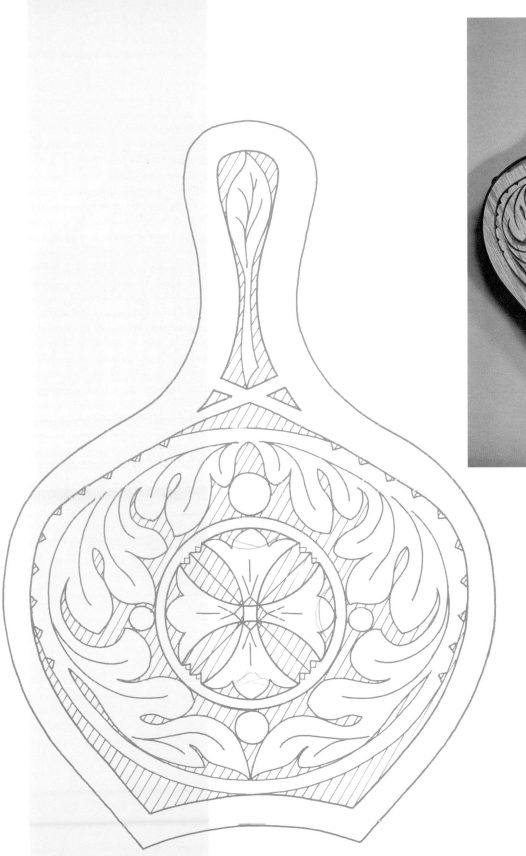

Butternut bellows,
12" × 8".

*12" scalloped,
beaded square
basswood plate.*

Peppermill,
4½" × 2½",
basswood.

Positive-image box lid pattern, 8⅜" × 5⅝".

Rosette detail of wall plaque.

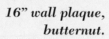

16" wall plaque, butternut.

Positive-image door panel pattern, 9" × 7½".

*Positive-image
floral pattern
for door panel.*

*6" scoop basswood plate
with positive-image trefoil.*

6" scoop basswood plate with positive-image trefoil.

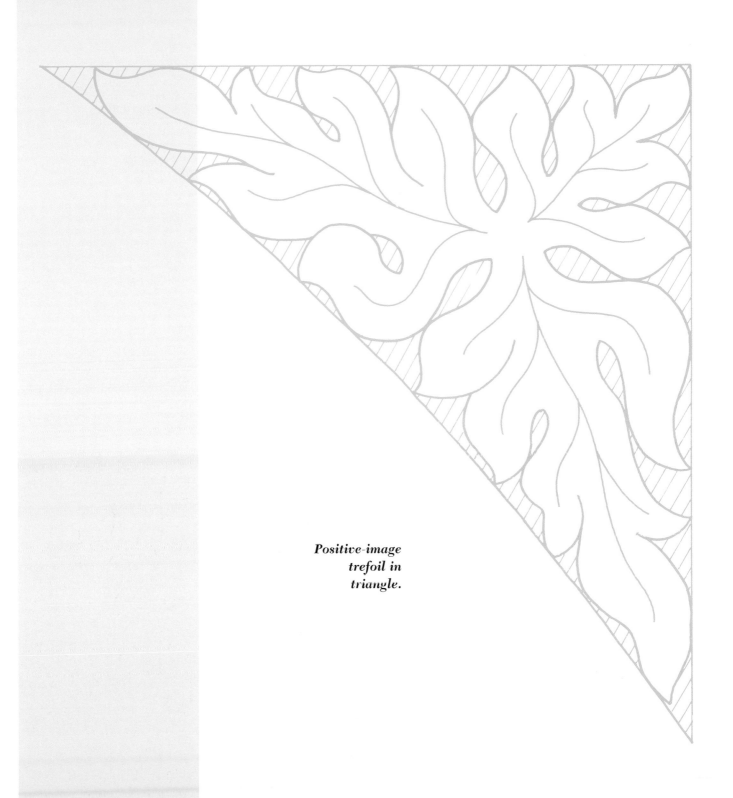

*Positive-image
trefoil in
triangle.*

Positive-image trefoil in rosette.

Positive-image leaf patterns for corners.

Box lid,
6¹¹⁄₁₆" × 9³⁄₈".

Basswood bench brush, 12" × 2½".

Positive-image leaf pattern.

Positive-image leaf pattern.

Positive-image trefoil on 8" plate plan.

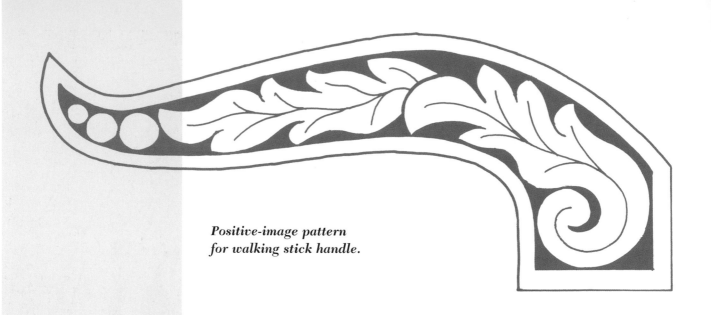

*Positive-image pattern
for walking stick handle.*

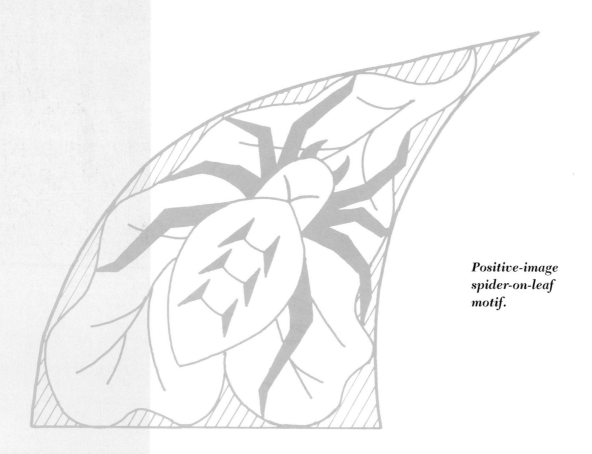

*Positive-image
spider-on-leaf
motif.*

Peppermill,
4½" × 2½",
basswood.

*Gothic cross,
14" × 9",
basswood.*

Sled, 17" × 7¼", white pine.

Top view of sled.

Positive-image leaf pattern for border.

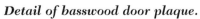

Detail of basswood door plaque.

(Nussbaum collection)

12" scalloped-rim basswood plate.

10" scalloped, beaded-rim basswood plate.

8"-rim basswood plate.

Free-Form Design

Free-form chip carving is a style that generally steers away from the geometrical. It is commonly used to depict natural forms such as animals, birds, flowers, and foliage. It is accomplished by incising the design into the wood rather than relieving the background, leaving a positive image.

Free-form motifs can be realistic or fanciful, symmetrical or irregular, simple or ornate. They can be combined with other design elements such as geometrical components and lettering. Because natural forms can be interpreted in so many different ways, free-form motifs offer a wonderful opportunity for a variety of interpretations.